Holiday Jokes for Kids 2

Jokes for New Year's, Valentine's Day, St. Patrick's Day and 4th of July

Sparky Riggs

FOREWARD

It's a common truth that it is harder to make people laugh than to make them cry. If you can make someone laugh then you have the ability to connect with each other in more meaningful, creative ways. The late Robin Williams once said *"I basically started performing for my mother going, "Love me!" What drives you to perform is the need for that primal connection. When I was little, my mother was funny with me, and I started to be charming and funny to her, and I learned that by being entertaining, you make a connection with another person."*

I'm a firm believer that a sense of humor is a quality that can be developed in children at an early age. Books like this one help kids explore the art of comedy and hopefully enable them to start building lifelong connections with others.

Keep on cracking those jokes!

-Sparky

CONTENTS

NEW YEAR'S DAY JOKES

In what place is New Year's Eve so mathematical?

Times Square

How did the child meet his New Year's Resolution of doing more reading for school?

He turned on the subtitles on the television

What happened to the person who stole a calendar on New Year's Eve?

He got 12 months

What did the dog have to say for New Year's resolutions?

I will not to bark when I see another dog

I will shake rainwater off of myself before I come in the house

I will not steal anyone's underwear

What was the shark's New Year's resolution?

To improve his public image

What is a New Year's Resolution?

A "To Do" list for the first week of January

What's a cow's favorite holiday?

Moo Year's Eve

What did the cheerleaders say on New Year's Day?

Happy New Cheer

Why did the girl sprinkle sugar on her pillow on New Year's Eve?

She wanted to start the year with sweet dreams

Knock Knock

Who's there?

Mary and Abby

Mary and Abby who?

Mary Christmas and Abby New Year

What do snowmen like to do on New Year's Eve?

Chill Out

What is corn's favorite holiday?

New EAR'S Day

What's the best New Year's resolution?

1080p

What should you never eat on New Year's Eve?

Fire crackers

What does a ghost say on New Year's?

Happy New Fear

Guess why I decided <u>not</u> to quit all of my bad habits for New Year's resolutions?

Because nobody likes a quitter

Why do you need a jeweler on New Year's Eve?

To ring in the new year

Why are there so many vampires out on New Year's Eve?

For Old Fangs Time

What party do snowmen attend on New Year's Eve?

The Snow Ball

What happened to the iPhone bully on New Year's Eve?

It was charged with battery

What happened to the fireworks who were arrested on New Year's Eve?

They were let off

What do you say to someone at midnight on New Year's Eve?

I haven't seen you since last year

What does a Ghost say on January 1st?

Happy BOO year

'

What is a New Year's resolution?

Something that goes in one year and out the other

Did you hear about Dracula missing the New Year's Ball?

There was a count down

Why do so many people smile in December?

It's The Most Wonderful Time of the Year

Why does the person who runs Time's Square on New Year's feel like a failure?

He always drops the ball

What do you say to the delivery guy who drops off your pizza after midnight on New Year's Eve?

I ordered this a year ago!

What did one snowman say to the other?

(Sniff, sniff)... Do you smell carrots?

Why did the police go to the daycare center on New Year's Eve?

It was naptime and someone was resisting a rest

How do an optimist and a pessimist ring in the New Year?

An optimist stays up until midnight to see the New Year in while a pessimist stays up to make sure the old year leaves

What happens the next day, if you accidentally eat a bunch of confetti?

You become a party pooper

How can you avoid taking your Christmas lights down on New Year's Day?

By turning your house into an Italian restaurant

Did you hear about the guy who started fixing breakfast on New Year's Eve?

He wanted to make a New Year's toast

What did the farmer give his wife on New Year's Eve?

Hogs and kisses

What did the little champagne bottle call his father?

Pop

VALENTINE'S DAY JOKES

What did Microsoft Windows™ say to his girlfriend?

Can I crash at your place tonight?

What did the man with the broken leg say to his nurse?

I've got a crutch on you

Did you hear about the romance in the tropical fish tank?

It was a case of guppy love

What do you call two birds in love?

Tweet-hearts

What do you call a very small Valentine?

A valen-tiny

Why did the boy put clothes on the Valentines he was sending?

Because they needed to be ad-dressed

Why do Valentines have hearts on them?

Because spleens would look pretty gross

What is the most romantic city in England?

Lover-pool

What did Frankenstein say to his girlfriend?

Be my valen-stein

Did you hear the one about the phony Cupid?

He was totally bow-gus

Why is Valentine's Day the best day for a celebration?

Because you can really party hearty

Why didn't Cupid shoot his arrow at the lawyer's heart?

Because even Cupid can't hit a target that small

What did one oar say to the other?

Can I interest you in a little row-mance?

Knock Knock

Who's there?

Olive

Oliver who?

Olive you and I don't care who knows it

What happened when the two angels got married?

They lived harp-ily ever after

Why should you never break up with a soccer goalie?

Because she's a keeper

Do you have a date for Valentine's Day?

Yes. It's February 14th

What would you get if you crossed Cupid with a baseball player?

A glover boy

What did the dog write on his Valentine card?

I drool-ly love you

Did Adam and Eve ever have a date?

No, they had an apple

What did the flame say to his buddies after he fell in love?

I found the perfect match

What did one pickle say to the other?

You mean a great dill to me

What did the painter say to her boyfriend on Valentine's Day?

I love you with all my art

How did the phone propose to his girlfriend on Valentine's Day?

He gave her a ring

What did the girl cat say to the boy cat on Valentine's Day?

You're purrr-fect for me

Where do all the hamburgers take their girlfriend on Valentine's Day?

To a Meat Ball

What Valentine's Day candy is best to give a girl?

Her-She Kisses

What kind of Valentine's Day candy is never on time?

Choco-LATE

What did Pilgrims give each other on Valentine's Day?

Mayflowers

What did one snake say to the other snake?

Give me a little hug and a hiss

What's the best part of Valentine's Day?

The day after when all the chocolate goes on sale

What did one font say to the other on Valentine's Day?

You're just my type

What food is crazy about Valentine's Day chocolates?

A cocoa-nut

ST. PATRICK'S DAY JOKES

What do you call an Irish spider?

A Paddy long legs

What's little and green and stuck to your bumper?

A leprechaun who didn't look both ways

Where would you find a leprechaun baseball team?

In the Little League

What do you call a leprechaun's vacation home?

A lepre-condo

What do you call a leprechaun with a sore throat?

A streprechaun

Are there many selfish people in Ireland?

Yes, because in Ireland, "I" always comes first

Why is Ireland the fastest growing country in Europe?

It's always Dublin

What do you call an Irishman in the knockout stages of soccer's World Cup?

A referee

Why did the Irish tenor stand on the chair?

So he could reach the high notes

Why can't you borrow money from a leprechaun?

Because they are always a little short

Knock Knock

Who's there?

Ireland

Ireland who?

Ireland you money if you promise to pay me back

What did one cook say about the other cook's Irish stew?

It could use a pinch of Gaelic

What do leprechauns love to barbecue?

Short ribs

Why are leprechauns so hard to get along with?

Because they're very short-tempered

What baseball position do leprechauns usually play?

Shortstop

Why are the Irish very concerned about global warming?

They are really into green living

Why do people wear shamrocks on St. Patrick's Day?

Because real rocks are too heavy

Why don't you iron a four-leaf clover?

Because you don't want to press your luck

What do you call a clumsy Irish dance?

A jig mistake

What do you call an Irishman who keeps bouncing off of walls?

Rick O'Shea

What would you get if you crossed a leprechaun with a Texan?

A pot of chili at the end of the rainbow

What do you get when two leprechauns have a conversation?

A lot of small talk

What's the best way to get a letter to Ireland?

Send it Eire mail

What would you get if you crossed a dog with a famous Irish actor?

Peter O'Drool

What did the leprechaun referee say when the soccer match ended?

Game clover

What would you get if you crossed an ignorant monster with Ireland's capital city?

Duh-blin

What would you get if you crossed a dog with an Irish instrument?

A bag-pup

Did you hear the one about the Irish peat?

You can dig it

When is an Irish potato not an Irish potato?

When it's a French fry

What would you get if you crossed a leprechaun with a frog?

A little green man with a croak of gold

What would you get if you crossed an Irishman with a basketball star?

Eire Jordan

What do you call a rainy day in Ireland?

A bad Eire day

What did the Irishman try to gamble with at the casino?

Potato chips

How did the leprechaun get to the moon?

In a sham rocket

What kind of music does a leprechaun band play?

Shamrock 'n' roll

Why did St. Patrick drive the snakes out of Ireland?

Because it was too far for them to crawl

What kind of spells do leprechaun witches cast?

Lucky Charms

What type of bow can't a leprechaun tie?

A rainbow

Why can't Irish golfers ever end a game?

They refuse to leave the green

How do you pay for soft drinks on St. Patrick's Day?

With soda bread

What should you say to a runner in the St. Patrick's Day marathon?

I-rish you luck

Why was St. Patrick given a desk job when he became a policeman?

He was too green to go out on patrol

Why were all the leprechauns still complaining in April about it raining on St. Patrick's Day?

Because the Irish stew

What do Irishmen say when you tell them Bono is your favorite singer?

You too?

Why do frogs like St. Patrick's Day?

Because they're already wearing green

4TH OF JULY JOKES

What would you get if you crossed the first signer of the Declaration of Independence with a rooster?

John Hancock-a-doodle-doo

What quacks, has webbed feet and betrays his country?

Bene-duck Arnold

Did you hear about the crooked George Washington?

He committed Valley Forgery

What protest by a group of dogs occurred in 1773?

The Boston Flea Party

What happened as a result of the Stamp Act?

The Americans licked the British

Why did Paul Revere ride his horse from Boston to Lexington?

Because the horse was too heavy to carry

Why did the British cross the Atlantic?

To get to the other tide

What would you get if you crossed a patriot with a small curly-haired dog?

Yankee Poodle

Did you hear the one about the Liberty Bell?

Yeah, it cracked me up

What would you get if you crossed George Washington with cattle feed?

The Fodder of Our Country

What did one flag say to the other flag?

Nothing. It just waved

What's red, white, black and blue?

Uncle Sam falling down the steps

Where did George Washington buy his hatchet?

At the chopping mall

What was General Washington's favorite tree?

The infantry

Which colonists told the most jokes?

Pun-sylvanians

What would you get if you crossed Washington's home with nasty insects?

Mt. Vermin

What did the patriot put on his dry skin?

Revo-lotion

Who is a dogs favorite Founding Father?

Bone Franklin

What dance was very popular in 1776?

Indepen-dance

Which one of Washington's officers was the biggest joker?

Laugh-ayette

What did Paul Revere say at the end of his ride?

I gotta get a softer saddle

Why did Washington chop down the cherry tree with his hatchet?

Because his mother wouldn't let him play with the chain saw

The Declaration of Independence was written in Philadelphia. True or false?

False! It was written in ink

What has four legs, a shiny nose, and fought for England?

Rudolph the Redcoat Reindeer

What would you get if you crossed a monster with a redcoat?

A bigger target

Why is the Liberty Bell like a dropped Easter egg?

Because they're both cracked

Who wrote "Oh say, can you see?"'

An eye doctor

What would you get if you crossed Patrick Henry with a hungry Italian boy?

A patriot who says, "Give me lasagna or give me death!"

What has feathers, webbed feet, and certain inalienable rights?

The Duck-laration of Independence

Why did the duck say "Bang!" on the 4th of July?

Because he was a fire quacker

What cat said, "The British are coming! The British are coming!"?

Paw Revere

What was the craziest battle of the Revolutionary War?

The Battle of Bonkers Hill

What was Thomas Jefferson's favorite dessert?

Monti-jello

What did King George think about the American colonists?

He thought they were revolting

Why were the early American settlers like ants?

Because they lived in colonies

How come there is no knock knock jokes about America?

Because freedom rings

Where was the Declaration of Independence signed?

On the bottom

Why does our country have a two-party system?

So we can have one party on Friday and one on Saturday

Why did Paul Revere take a midnight ride?

Because he missed the 10:30 bus

What would you get if you crossed a vegetable with the first president of the United States?

George Squash-ington

How did the Founding Father's decide on our nation's flag?

They took a flag poll

What would you get if you crossed the American national bird with Snoopy?

A bald beagle

What did the visitor say as he left the Statue of Liberty?

Keep in torch

What's big, cracked, and carries your luggage?

The Liberty Bellhop

What ghost haunted King George III?

The spirit of '76

Did you hear about the cartoonist in the Continental Army?

He was a Yankee doodler

What's the difference between a duck and George Washington?

One has bill on his face and the other has his face on a bill

What do you eat on the 5th of July?

Independence Day old macaroni salad

Why does the Statue of Liberty stand?

Because she can't sit down

What did the four-year old say when his mother said that our soldiers fought so that you could be free?

I'm not free, I'm four

What did the police do when they arrested a battery and a firework?

They charged one and let the other one off

What did one firecracker say to the other firecracker?

My pop is bigger than your pop

Do other countries have a 4th of July?

Yes. It always comes right after July 3rd

What did the colonists wear to the Boston Tea Party?

Tea-shirts

Made in the USA
San Bernardino, CA
09 February 2020

64223018R00044